Surviving Twenties

A Survival Guide for Early Twentysomethings

Bria Aleisha

Copyright © 2021 Bria Whitehurst All rights reserved

The characters and events portrayed in this book are fictitious. Any similarity to real persons, living or dead, is coincidental and not intended by the author.

No part of this book may be reproduced, or stored in a retrieval system, or transmitted in any form or by any means, electronic, mechanical, photocopying, recording, or otherwise, without express written permission of the publisher.

ISBN-13: 978-0-578-80027-1

Cover design & Interior Formatting by: Bria Aleisha
Printed in the United States of America

Dedications

This book is dedicated to my family who has provided me with unconditional love and support. To my boyfriend Quenton, thank you for helping my vision come true. To all the early 20somethings who feel like no one truly understand their struggle. I want you to know that I hear you, I see you, and I feel your pain. You will get through the adversity you are encountering, because you are a survivor!

Contents

Introduction	6
Welcome to adulthood	1
Comparison	9
Finances	18
Relationships	25
Mid-Twenties	38
Surviving Twenties	41
About the Author	45

Introduction

Hello! My name is Bria Aleisha, just like yourself I am a twentysomething. I am the founder and creator of Surviving Twenties and Surviving Twenties Podcast. At the age of twenty-six, I was experiencing a quarter-life-crisis. My life was not reflecting the timeline I created for myself. I was still living at my parent's house, working at a low paying job, but hey at least it was in my field. I was in graduate school to obtain another degree, while getting over a heartbreak from an on-again-off-again college sweetheart. I was constantly asking myself where did I go wrong? I mean thirty was around the corner, I thought I was doing everything the "right way." In therapy, is where I came to the conclusion that I am really surviving my twenties.

During therapy, for me, surviving twenties meant challenging my thoughts and behaviors pertaining to every aspect of my life. First, I had to detach myself from the false reality that I created in my head as to how my life should be. Next, I learned to let go of toxic behaviors, relationships, and friendships that was no longer serving a purpose in my life. That also involved taking accountability for my actions because let's face it, I'm not always right. Lastly, giving myself grace, being gentle and patient with myself because it's unrealistic to think I would have life figured out before turning thirty.

While in therapy I developed a survival kit. A survival kit which consisted of tools and healthy coping mechanisms that I utilized to help overcome obstacles in my life. In my survival kit are prayer, therapy, friends, family, and exercising.

My journey throughout my twenties inspired me to create a safe space online where twentysomethings are able to express themselves freely without feeling judged or alone. To have a sense of community with other twentysomethings to normalize and celebrate the trials and adversities we encounter and overcome.

Surviving Twenties

Welcome to adulthood

Welcome to adulthood! Adulthood is a fun and terrifying journey you'll experience around the tender age of twenty. Early adulthood is a time of self-exploration, discovering your identity, sexuality, and figuring out the person you want to become. Your early twenties are an exciting time where you are able to experience life through your own lens on your terms. There is no reason to rush this phase of your life.

It would be improbable to believe you should have your entire life planned out or hell even the next month for that matter. Usually around this time we have created a timeline for ourselves as to how our life will turn out, but we will get to that later in the book. What you can expect from this survival guide are tools and tips to help you create your own personal survival kit to use when you are encountering challenges in your life. The book you are now reading is dedicated to the early twentysomethings that are literally trying to figure life out.

Bria Aleisha

Pipe Dream

Growing up, I was taught that I needed to have a plan for my life. In fact, the only way to become successful is by planning ahead. The infamous "plan" was to graduate from high school, attend college, graduate college within four years, and gain employment within my field. Does this plan sound familiar?

The issue I have with the "plan", is this plan is not the only way to succeed. The plan creates an illusion that you will be exempt from failure and disappointment as long as you follow this specific path. The plan does not leave room for flexibility or discovery. The plan is quite frankly a pipe dream. Yes, I dare say a pipe dream.

A pipe dream that is instilled in us at a young age and reinforced throughout our schooling. Eventually leading us to create false expectations and timelines as to how our life should go. I am not opposed to this plan. However, it's just not realistic for everyone. Let's face it, college is not for everyone and honestly it does not equate to success most of the time.

There are so many twentysomethings that are enrolling in undergraduate and graduate school, because they feel

Surviving Twenties

pressured to follow this plan or because this plan provides a sense of security.

For me personally, following this plan provided me with a sense of security, familiarity, and debt. I believed that I was in control because I knew what to expect and what was expected of me during my academic career.

In college I felt safe because, as long as I continued to do what was required of me then everything should fall into place, right?

My freshman year of college I began to "should myself". Yes, you read that correctly, I began to should myself. Let me explain to you what "shoulding" is. Shoulding is placing expectations or obligations on yourself and others based on what you believe should happen. Throughout college, I created several "I should" statements. My "I should" statements looked somewhat like this during college:

    By my sophomore year I *should* join a sorority.

    I *should* have a job before graduating college.

    I *should* have an apartment after college.

My boyfriend *should* propose to me at college graduation.

Bria Aleisha

Timeline

My "I should" statements" began to morph into a timeline that I envisioned for my life. My timeline made me feel like I was adulting. I had specific plans and goals that I wanted to accomplish before turning thirty. Thirty is the marker of success for most twentysomethings. Thirty is considered a milestone.

That moment in life when you transition into a more mature version of adulthood. The last thing I wanted to be was in my thirties wishing I had accomplished more in my twenties.

<u>Bria's timeline</u>

I will work within my field after college graduation.

I will start and graduate from graduate school by the age of twenty-five.

I will become a homeowner by the age of twenty-seven.

I will have my first kid at the age of twenty-nine.

I will be engaged and married before the age of thirty.

Surviving Twenties

After college graduation, I tried my hardest to make my timeline become a reality. My college sweetheart broke up with me a few days after graduation, so there went the marriage and kids. In August 2014, I gained employment within my field, however, I was terminated after my first ninety days. Then, to top it off I was unable to start graduate school the following Fall semester after graduation.

I felt like a failure, I was living back home with my parents and working at Kids Foot Locker with a Bachelor of Science in Psychology. This is the part of adulthood no one prepared us for. The disappointments of life. Life's uncertainties will manage to disrupt the timeline of the life we envision for ourselves. This leaves twentysomethings confused and frustrated regarding what to do next.

We began to personalize and internalize life's misfortunes equating the setbacks to our self-worth. Self-doubt begins to creep in resulting in most twentysomethings questioning their own abilities. Guilt begins to fester generating an internal dialogue of what you should have done differently. Those "I should" statements and the timeline have now created a breeding ground for depression and anxiety. The disappointment phase of adulthood seems

Bria Aleisha

impossible to overcome. To overcome this phase, you will need your first survival tool perception.

Survival Tool: Perception

Perception is a powerful tool to utilize when experiencing uncertainties in life. Your perception influences your reality and the world around you. How you perceive your current situation is detrimental as to how you will defeat it. To better understand your perception, requires a certain level of awareness to determine what your perception is rooted in. In our early twenties our perception is deeply rooted in expectations. Sadly, expectations and reality contradict one another. Therefore, establishing a timeline will do more harm than good. Although, throughout our life we are taught to have a plan. However, we cannot allow the plan to control our life or influence our perception as to how life should be. A part of adulting is putting things into perspective.

Surviving Twenties

Putting things into perspective looks like this:
Accepting your reality for what it is.
Focusing on what you know to be true.
Reflecting on your accomplishments.
Managing your expectations.
Limiting your "I should" statements.
Surrounding yourself with positive people.
Reminding yourself this phase in your life is a season not a lifetime.

As you progress in your twenties, keeping an open perspective will strengthen you mentally and help you adjust to life challenges better. If you are struggling with changing your perception, here are some questions to ask yourself.

Bria Aleisha

Questions

How do you perceive yourself?

Is the perception of yourself positive or negative? Why or why not?

What is your perception rooted in (expectations, past trauma, other's expectations)?

Is your situation(s) affecting your self-perception?

Is your current perception helping or hindering your situation?

What are ways you can change your perception?

Surviving Twenties

Comparison

Social Comparison

Now that you have your first survival tool, perception, let's discuss how comparison can also be rooted in our perception. Social comparison appears throughout our life in many forms and facets. Social comparison can motivate us to thrive to accomplish our goals because we have seen others accomplish their goals. Comparing ourselves to others can be reassuring at times, especially when a person is worse off than us. Although, I did not have a job immediately after I graduated from college.

I would always make myself feel better by saying "at least I graduate within four years unlike my friends."

Comparison may appear as a harmless act that everyone does either intentionally or unintentionally. However, when we begin to compare and measure ourselves to others, our self-perception begins to change. We began to associate our value with others by comparing our journey to theirs. Idealizing the person and making them our standard, which can cause us to lose our sense of identity.

Bria Aleisha

Social comparison can have twentysomethings perceiving themselves as inadequate and unsuccessful. When early twentysomethings are unable to achieve the similar results that others have accomplished. Unwanted feelings of envy and jealousy may begin to develop. Resulting in twentysomethings believing they are running out of time to complete their goals. Like there is an invisible hourglass that rapidly counts down the remaining time you have left to become successful.

Social Media

Social Media exacerbates negative social comparison. We spend countless hours watching others display their best version of their life on social media convincing us that's their reality. Let me kick some game to you quickly, you cannot compare an individual's social media highs to your real-life lows. In other words, people are only showing you what they want you to see. No one is posting their failures, so why are you comparing yourself to a false reality?

Let's play devil advocate, say if the person who you are comparing yourself to is accomplishing their goals on and off social media. You do not know the struggles they may have endured to reach the level of success they have

Surviving Twenties

reached. You are only seeing a glimpse of their life. I have noticed that twentysomethings, myself included, tend to compare ourselves in these areas on social media:

Graduating on time.

Relationship goals.

Being married by a certain age.

Becoming employed.

Becoming a homeowner.

Becoming an entrepreneur.

Traveling

Appearance

As a recent college graduate, seeing others post their achievements on social media made me feel inadequate. I started to feel as if I was the only one struggling, while everybody else was living their best life. I began to ask myself "what is wrong with me?" and "why can't I seem to get it right?" I was attaching my self-worth to the lack of success I had in my life. I wanted a house, the dream job, the relationship, and to travel the world too.

 I was so consumed with what others were doing, I became less motivated to achieve my own dreams. I did not realize I was in the cycle of comparison.

Bria Aleisha

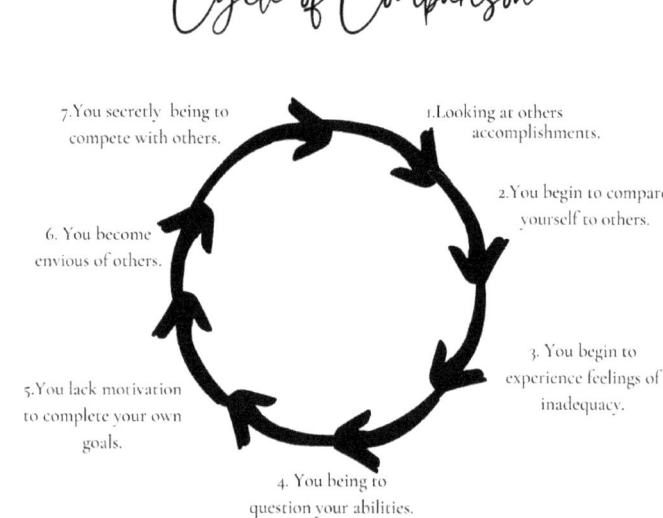

I began to speak negatively about myself. I would make statements like:

I will never get a job in my field.

There must be something wrong with me because, I'm single.

I will never be able to move out of my parents' house.

This degree doesn't mean anything.

Surviving Twenties

While being in the vicious cycle of comparison, it became difficult for me to appreciate my own accolades. It was not until my mentor texted me saying she was proud of me. With a confused look on my face, I responded "Why are you proud of me? I haven't done anything but struggle since graduating from college." She replied, reminding me of all my achievements and encouraged me to practice gratitude. My mentor explained to me that my journey is uniquely tailored to me.

Therefore, I must trust myself and the process. Trusting the process meant believing that things would get better despite my current situation. To help combat comparison your next set of tools are awareness and gratitude.

Survival Tools: Self-awareness and Gratitude
In the survival kit, I imagined perception as the hammer, self-awareness and gratitude are the nails that you use to conjoin things together. In other words, self-awareness, perception, and gratitude combined can help eliminate comparison. Comparison is an act triggered by external factors resulting in internal conflicts with one's self. Practicing self-awareness provides you with insight about yourself to ensure that your thoughts, emotions and behavior are aligning with your authentic self.

Bria Aleisha

Self-awareness helps eliminate comparison because you become more mindful of how comparing yourself affects you emotionally, mentally and physically. Is comparing yourself aligning up with your authentic self? No, it's not. Therefore, you have to become aware of when you are comparing yourself and what triggers these comparisons.

Here are ways to practice self-awareness:
Acknowledge your feelings.

Keep a reflection journal.

Be mindful of what bothers you.

Write down how you are feeling and the thoughts you are experiencing.

Have an accountability partner that will hold you accountable when you are not being your authentic self. Self-awareness and perception are deeply intertwined with one another. Self-awareness acknowledges and processes your internal self, while your perception processes the world around you. Utilizing both tools simultaneously help you address how you are feeling while putting things into perspective. For example, when one of my followers on Instagram posted a picture about becoming a homeowner. I became envious because I felt that I should become a homeowner.

Surviving Twenties

The feelings of envy were rooted in my desire to become a homeowner and seeing someone else achieving a personal goal of mine. By putting things into perspective, I had to look at the bigger picture. At the age of 23, I was not ready to purchase a home. I barely had $500 to my name. I reminded myself that when I saw my followers post their success on Instagram, that was motivation for me to continue to persevere. On the next page are questions to help you practice self-awareness while putting things into perspective

Bria Aleisha

Questions

What are areas in your life do you compare with others? What are your comparison triggers?

What emotions/thoughts does your comparison trigger evoke inside of you?

The emotions/thoughts you are experiencing are what are they rooted in?

What are ways you can put into perspective?

Surviving Twenties

As twentysomethings we tend to look outward to confirm our feelings of self-worth and happiness. Gratitude helps you break out of the comparison cycle. Gratitude is an intentional act of being thankful for what you have and practicing thankfulness.

Here are ways to practice gratitude:

Identify three to five thing you love about yourself.
Identify three things you are grateful for
Write gratitude notes.
Practice gratitude affirmations.

Now that you have your three survival tools Gratitude, Perception, and Self-awareness these can be seen as your G.P.S., your moral compass to help navigate through life and life challenges.

Bria Aleisha

Finances

More Money, More Problems
A part of becoming an adult is managing your finances. Managing your money can be intimidating if you are always robbing Peter to pay Paul. There is a common misconception that if you make more money than you will be able to afford all your bills. We all know how the saying goes "more money means mean problems" especially when you do not know how to manage your finances. In our early twenties we all make financial mistakes.

Whether that is taking extra student loans out to receive a refund check in college, applying for multiple credit cards, or emotional spending. Managing your finances can seem impossible when you don't have a steady stream of income. So, you are probably wondering what it takes to manage your finances or how the older generation could make twenty dollars stretch for a week.

Surviving Twenties

The key to managing your finances is having healthy financial habits and financial goals. Financial habits are habits that dictate how you spend your money. A financial goal is an ideal target you set for yourself to help achieve financial stability, whether it is to purchase an item or save. To achieve your financial goal(s) requires a budget.

Budget
A budget brings awareness to how and where you spend your money. Within your budget it is best to include your current income, top financial priorities (rent, cell phone, tuition, grocery, etc.) and your wants. When creating your budget, list when you receive your income (refund check, check, money from family, etc) and the dates of your bills. This will help you remember when everything is due. Once you calculate your expenses, the money that is remaining can be deposited into your savings or it becomes your allowance.

Bria Aleisha

Every twentysomethings needs an emergency savings whether big or small. We all know that life can and will come at us fast! Having an emergency savings help provide a sense of security to cover those unexpected expenses. An emergency savings is only meant to be used for emergencies, not when you do not have any money. If you are unable to pay yourself or save because the majority of your money is going to bills, do not guilt yourself.

Review your bill, necessities, and wants to determine what you can live without. Do you really need every streaming service subscription such as Apple, Hulu, HBO Max, and Netflix? Do you need to get your nails and your feet done every two weeks? Can you skip going to the barber shop/hair salon weekly/ bi-weekly?

Once you are comfortable with your budget, your next step is to PAY YOUR BILLS. Do not hesitate to pay your bills on time. Do not use the money for your rent or utility money to go shopping, for the club, or lend to friends/family members. If you receive a refund check while in school manage your money wisely. Do not request several student loans solely to get a refund check.

Surviving Twenties

If you have a credit card, please do not pay the minimum on your credit card. Making these financial mistakes can have a lasting impact on your credit score.

In college, I did not have a car, I created healthy financial habits and a financial goal to save three thousand dollars as a down payment for a car. I created a budget to help determine how much I could save. My budget consisted of all my expenses and income.

My income covered my expenses, however, I still made financial scarifies. Some of the financial sacrifices I made were renting textbooks instead of buying them, living on campus, cutting out fast food, and not going out as often. Becoming aware of where I spent my money and how much money I spent was my main priority. While in college, I worked at the school cafeteria, I got paid bi-weekly and my check were $300-$500. My second check of each month I was able to save $200 a month for the remaining of my sophomore year. In the fall semester of my junior year, I was able to purchase my car.

Bria Aleisha

Being a good steward over your money is possible, regardless of your financial situation. Remember, money is a tool, you have to take ownership of your money and make it work for you. Increasing your awareness of how you spend your money, where you spend your money, and when you spend your money is essential.

I encourage you to begin budgeting and to establish healthy financial habits and financial goals. It doesn't matter the amount, starting will help you achieve financial stability in the long run. It's a marathon, not a sprint. To help you understand your relationship with money, answer the questions on the next page.

Surviving Twenties

Questions

What is your current relationship with money?

What is your perception of money?

Fill in the blank " I spend money when I feel _____?"

Do you spend the majority of your money on pleasures or necessities?

Do you spend money to avoid addressing your emotions/feelings?

In the past thirty days, how many times did your money spend impulsively?

Bria Aleisha

Survival Tool: Disciplined
Adjusting to budgeting requires a new survival tool, disciplined. Becoming disciplined with your finances will help you create financial freedom and financial independence for the future. Holding yourself accountable will reduce your likelihood of spending impulsively, unexpected bills, and increasing debt. Your money becomes more flexible and you are able to spend your money how you please without feeling guilty. Honestly, being discipline can help you in different areas in your life.

To become self-disciplined, create small goals and work towards achieving them. For example, make a goal to set aside five dollars every time you get paid. Or make it a priority to get off of social media at a certain time each day. Becoming self-disciplined helps develop your inner strength.

Surviving Twenties

Relationships

Self-Love

In our twenties relationships with our family, friends, and significant others have a great influence on our lives. The most important relationship of them all, is the relationship we have with ourselves. The relationship you have with yourself sets the tone for your relationships with others. Having a relationship with yourself may seem taboo because in our early twenties our focus is on creating our tribe and fostering relationships. Being a relationship with yourself does not equate to loneliness and this is coming from a twentysomething who struggled with being alone. Just like most twentysomethings the fear of being alone is frightening. However, you are not alone, you are with yourself. A relationship with yourself teaches you how to be comfortable with yourself, self-love, and how you want to be treated by others. If you are unsure on how to initiate a relationship with yourself, try these tips.

Bria Aleisha

Here are ways to practice self-love:
Be gentle with yourself.
Write yourself a love letter.
Take yourself on a date.
Spend time alone doing your favorite hobby.

Your Tribe

Finding your tribe is the most exciting time in your early twenties. As your life begins to transition, so do your friends. Unfortunately, your childhood friends are not as visible or relevant as they once were. You are establishing new friendships with individuals that you share commonalities with. Everyone seems like your new best friend; but remember Meek Mills said it best there are levels to this.

There are levels to friendships. The harsh reality of friendships is realizing everyone you consider to be a friend does not always view you as the same way. Some people are only around you because you are accessible. They like to take but never reciprocate. While others befriend you to secretly compete with you. When you are unsure about where you stand in a friendship take inventory by asking yourself the following questions.

Surviving Twenties

Questions

Is this friendship beneficial to my life? Why or why not?

Does this friend bring drama or peace to my life?

Do I find myself avoiding this particular friend?

Can I trust this friend with specific details of my life?

Has this relationship with my friend(s) become one-sided?

Am I being the friend, I desire my friend(s) to be to me? Why or why not?

Bria Aleisha

Relationship

Dating in our early twenties is so complex because no one knows what they want exactly. Some will say they are looking for a good time, while others are enjoying the vibe. Long story short some twentysomething want relationship benefits without the relationship. In an ideal world this is an ambiguous relationship that is commonly known as a situationship or entanglement. A situationship/entanglement is a sexual relationship between two individuals who are not interested in having a committed relationship. The individuals have a mutual understanding that the relationship is entirely based upon sexual interaction, no feelings involved. The downside of a situtionship or entanglement is someone will develop feelings, resulting in the individual feeling entitled to relationship's privileges.

If you know that you desire a relationship, do not entertain the thought of being in a situationship. There is a small chance the situationship/entanglement will morph into a relationship, but do you really want to be in a relationship with someone you had to force into a relationship?

Surviving Twenties

If you are a twentysomething who desires to be in a relationship, establish the type of relationship that you want to be in. Define how you want to be dated. Make a true effort to get to know the person you are interested in. Sadly, dating has become texting, communicating on social media, and hanging out from time to time. Do not be ashamed of being intentional about dating. Be mindful of red flags when getting to know a person.

The red flags are warning signs that are foreshadowing that this could lead to problems in the future. Here are the most common red flags to be mindful of.

Bria Aleisha

Red Flags

This person ghosts you frequently.

This person gaslights you.

This person is extremely jealous when you are around others.

This person attempts to isolate you from others.

This person is emotionally abusive in a passive aggressive manner.

This person blames you for everything.

This person disregards your feelings.

Surviving Twenties

Through my college career I was in a toxic relationship. My relationship was on again and off again. One minute we would be perfectly fine then the next we would be cursing one another out. However, I knew for a fact that he was one. I was so fixated on being his main girl, I tolerated an enormous amount of disrespect.

My focus was on my relationship and my relationship only; that my grades and health were affected. I had several encounters with other females because of my boyfriend (who didn't attend the university by the way). One incident in particular resulted in me going to the Dean office of the university. I was at risk of being expelled from school, if I had another confrontation with the said persons. I started to hate the person I was becoming and resenting my boyfriend. I had to make a hard decision either choose myself or lose somewhat of the relationship I had. During my junior year of college, I decided to choose me. I began to date other people, my now ex-boyfriend at the time decided to remain cordial. However, my ex-boyfriend and I salvaged our relationship and began dating again my senior year.

Bria Aleisha

We both discussed what we wanted in the relationship and he promised to remain faithful. Although we were able maintain a healthy relationship, my boyfriend broke up with me because he no longer felt the same way I did. If you are currently in a relationship in your early twenties, be mindful that your significant other may or may not become your future wife or husband. When you are in love or infatuated with your partner it's common to envision sharing your life with them. You began to make plans for how you and your partner's life will turn out. Consuming yourself with the idea of what life could be like with your partner is dangerous because you are putting your faith in unrealistic expectations.

Focusing solely on the life you want with your partner can impede your judgement. You began to ignore red flags. You start tolerating things you normally would not for the sake of the relationship (i.e., disrespect, infidelity, abuse). Your self-identity is enmeshed within the relationship. You no longer have an identity outside your relationship. You stop doing the things that matter to you. You find yourself making sacrifices while your partner is not reciprocating the same energy and effort you have made towards the relationship.

Surviving Twenties

Again, there is nothing wrong with wanting to create a life with your current partner. There should be a mutual understanding about what you both want in the relationship. This goes back to utilizing your tools perception and awareness.

As time progresses within your relationship, re-evaluate with your partner the relationship. You may foresee the relationship being long-term. Although, you partner may feel otherwise.

Family

Just like your friendship dynamics changes, the dynamics of your relationships with your family members will change too. Family has a tendency of viewing twentysomethings as the children we once were. At times the expectation and values family members have are placed upon us causing conflict within the relationship. It is difficult being a young adult trying to find your voice without being perceived as being disrespectful or ungrateful. My mother and I had several disagreements and arguments throughout my college career.

Bria Aleisha

She had a version of me in her mind, while I was living another in real life. There was a disconnect between who I was as her daughter and the woman that I was becoming. In my early twenties, I was unable to communicate to my mother how I truly felt and how I preferred to approach things. I found myself trying to live up to her expectations in fear that if I did not, I would disappoint her.

Attempting to live up to my mother's expectations affected how I made decisions and caused conflict in my intimate relationship. I was in a constant state of war with myself. Moving back home after graduating from college gave me the courage, I needed to have a discussion with my parents. Although, the conversation did not go as smoothly as I intended. We were able to establish a mutual understanding about our relationship, the young woman I was becoming, and boundaries. Managing relationships whether it's family, friendships, or significant ant other requires two more survival tools: discernment and boundaries.

Surviving Twenties

Survival Tool: Discernment and Boundaries

Fostering a relationship with others requires discernment and boundaries. Discernment is the ability to decipher or judge well based upon what's being presented to you. Whether it is good or bad, discernment provides the insight to accept the person or situation for what is. We all have a level of discernment within us. Some people refer to discernment as the "gut feeling".

The gut feeling can be described as the feeling you experience forewarning you that something good or bad is going to happen. Or when you meet someone for the first time, you realize something about the person is not quite right, but you cannot put your finger on it. Yes, that your discernment or your gut feeling speaking to you, listen to it.

To increase your level of discernment, first be honest and accept the person and circumstances. Secondly, reflect on your judgment to help determine the best route to take. Lastly, adjust accordingly to the circumstances at hand. Utilizing discernment within your relationships will help you establish appropriate boundaries with others.

Bria Aleisha

Boundaries are guidelines or limits that are set in place to help you protect and honor yourself. There are different types of boundaries: emotional, physical, sexual, and financial. The boundaries you create for yourself are a reflection of what you are and are not willing to tolerate. Remember your boundaries are not solely for others to respect but are for you to respect as well. Here are examples of emotional, physical, sexual, and financial boundaries.

Surviving Twenties

Emotional Boundary	Physical Boundary
I would prefer for you not to use that tone because it's condescending and offensive.	I would prefer for you not touch me in that manner, it makes me uncomfortable.
Sexual Boundary	**Financial Boundary**
I would prefer to wait to discuss being intimate with one another until the relationship become serious.	I would prefer to not lend you any money until you are financial capable of paying me back.

Bria Aleisha

Mid-Twenties

Congratulations! You survived your early twenties. Remember how you felt when you first became a twentysomething. Now look at you! Adjusting and navigating adulthood like a pro, while managing self-care and implementing boundaries. Now you are getting ready to embark on another phase of life we like to call the mid-twenties.

Your mid-twenties will be similar to your early twenties, just more awkward. You are in the phase of feeling too old for the college kids but not old enough to hang with the older crowd. During this phase is when most twentysomething experience a quarter life crisis. Twentysomethings are asking themselves, am I doing this the right way?

Quarter-life-crisis typically occur during the mid-twenties because everything seems uncertain and unstable.

Friendships, relationships, and careers are changing. The habits you had in your early twenties are not conducive to your current stage of life. It appears that you are unsure where you "fit in" or if you're adulting correctly.

However, let's not forget you are fully equipped to handle

Surviving Twenties

this new phase of life because you have your survival tools.

Survival Tools

Perception: For better insight as to how you are viewing the world.

Self-Awareness: To be cognizant of your emotions, feelings, and behavior being your authentic self.

Gratitude: To always remember to be thankful for where you are in life and what you have.

Discipline: For self-regulating and control.

Discernment: The ability to judge, accept, and understand situations and people for their truths.

Boundaries: Having boundaries to protect yourself and others.

Bria Aleisha

Reflection

I hope throughout this journey of surviving your early twenties, the tools listed are helpful. In addition, you are able to develop and identify more survival tools. Remember you are not alone, on your journey of surviving your twenties. Below are reflection questions.

What are you learning/unlearning about yourself as an early twentysomething?

What are you currently surviving in your early twenties?

Are the survival tools helping you adjust to adulthood?

What survival tools have you added in your survival kit?

What does surviving your early twenties mean to you?

Surviving Twenties

Surviving Twenties

On Instagram and on the podcast Surviving Twenties is notorious for asking twentysomethings what surviving twenties means to them and what is in their survival kit. Here's what Surviving Twenties means to our followers.

"Surviving 20's means leaning on my friends, family, and a therapist and knowing that these tough weeks and months are only temporary! The items I used the most in my survival kit are my essential oils and tons of coffee. Those two are powerhouses and something I rely on every day to get me going."-@taynewman

"Surviving Twenties means building community and cultivating positive relationships. In my survival kit, is practicing self-reflection and being present."-@flacka0284

"Surviving 20's means to me, not just enduring the hardship of your 20's but also making the absolute best of it. In my survival kit would include a support network of people I trust, my passion, and knowledge for succeeding such as financial knowledge and books."-iminmytwenties

Bria Aleisha

"Surviving your 20's means finding your purpose and what you want out of life. Growing into the adult you desire to be. In my survival kit are faith, accountability, and praying."-@r0d.ney

"Surviving Twenties to me is like being on a roller coaster of ups, downs, twists, and turns. One minute it's scary; and the next it's amazing. It's a trial and error. Learning to unlearn a mindset that was conditioned from a different generation. Just learn from your mistakes, laugh, and never let anyone steal your joy. Life is hard, but so are you."-@versatilesheis

"Surviving Twenties means accepting losses as something that is necessary for growth. Stop rushing my timeline of success, stop comparing my life to others, and removing the limitations I have on God and make room for him to bless me with more than I could ever imagine. In my survival kit is Jesus, supportive people, dancing, music, drawing, and self-care."-@merilynshanell

"Surviving Twenties means to me following my true passion with an unapologetic attitude. It also means loving, taking care of myself and accepting me for me"-@dominiquemotivates

Surviving Twenties

"Surviving Twenties to me is your trial-and-error years. Things will happen, change, go wrong, etc. You will smile as well as cry a lot. You will quickly realize the life you always imagined may not be that imaginary timeline you set as a kid and that's okay. The years you'll gain strength, knowledge, and wisdom. You'll soon realize that you should live life for yourself and nobody else. Make yourself happy."-@brittneycox

"Surviving Twenties to me means surviving boot camp into adulthood. I feel that my twenties are preparing me for every possible thing adulthood has to offer. It's navigating the complexities and "I don't knows" in which will come with powerful lessons later."-@leaveinspired

"Surviving Twenties means to me following my true passion with an unapologetic attitude. It also means loving, taking care of myself and accepting me for me"-@dominiquemotivates

"Surviving Twenties means to me giving yourself grace because you don't know what to expect and as long as you try your best that's all you can give yourself."-alieshaadventures

Bria Aleisha

"Surviving twenties means surrendering to your past and idealized future and opening up to life it's experiences, realizing that it's all rigged in your favor. Also, that there is enough love, success, opportunity, wealth and health for everyone and there's no need to be in competition with anyone around you but yourself."- @evanbernad_

"Surviving Twenties learning to be okay with decisions that were best for me and not others and trusting myself to make the right decisions for me. In my survival kit, there's God, therapy, writing, and my support system."- @writefullysobrittany

"Surviving Twenties means to me finding peace. Finding meaning within. Living life with lessons learned instead of regrets. Setting goals and flourishing."-@tierrakj

About the Author

Bria Aleisha, MSW, LMSW, LCSW-A, is a Master Level Social Worker licensed in the state of North and South Carolina. Bria is the founder and creator of Surviving Twenties and Surviving Twenties Podcast with Bria Aleisha, LMSW. Bria is dedicated to empowering young adults in their twenties adjust and navigate their adulthood through her coaching services and podcast.

Bria Aleisha

www.ingramcontent.com/pod-product-compliance
Lightning Source LLC
Chambersburg PA
CBHW071514150426
43191CB00009B/1528